Original title:
A Symphony of Laughter and Love

Copyright © 2024 Creative Arts Management OÜ
All rights reserved.

Author: Colin Leclair
ISBN HARDBACK: 978-9916-94-338-0
ISBN PAPERBACK: 978-9916-94-339-7

## The Amplitude of Our Laughter

With chuckles that bounce, our spirits soar,
Jokes fly like confetti, laughter galore.
A pie in the face, what a glorious sight,
We twirl 'round the room, hearts feeling so light.

The tickle of wit, it dances on air,
Every quip and pun lightens our share.
Giggles erupt like balloons on a spree,
In this playful realm, we're wild and free.

## **The Dance of Our Delight**

With each little stumble, we rise with a grin,
In this silly waltz, you know it's a win.
Step on my toes, oh, what a surprise,
As laughter spills out, it brightens our eyes.

Around and around, we spin like a top,
Holding on tight, we never will stop.
Your smile shines bright, like a star in the night,
Together we move, everything feels right.

## **Colorful Echoes of Joy**

In a world painted bright, our laughter rings clear,
Echoing memories that bring us great cheer.
Witty remarks fly like kites on a breeze,
Here in this moment, we do as we please.

Rainbows of humor stretch wide in the sky,
Playful and vibrant, no reason to sigh.
With each burst of laughter, a color appears,
A canvas of joy, washed clean of our fears.

## The Gallop of Joyful Hearts

On ponies of laughter, we gallop along,
With whimsical beats, we dance to our song.
Each whoop and each snort, a pure joy parade,
In this light-hearted realm, we're never afraid.

Oh, the races we run, with giggles in tow,
Hurdles we leap, with a wink and a glow.
Our hearts, like fireworks, ignite in the dusk,
In this lively adventure, it's love that we trust.

## Harmonies of Happiness

In a world where silliness reigns,
Joy bubbles up like fizzy trains.
Giggles dance in a quirky beat,
Life's whimsy makes each day sweet.

Tickles float on a summer breeze,
Laughter sparkles among the trees.
Mismatched socks and playful pranks,
We smile wide, give goofy thanks.

Whispers shared over silly puns,
Collecting joy just like we run.
Balloons with faces, laughter flies,
In this joy, our spirit ties.

So come, dear friend, let's clown around,
In giggles, love is truly found.
With every chuckle, hearts will soar,
Together, funny is our core.

## The Chorus of Togetherness

Caffeine spills and morning's hue,
Slippers slip as we chase the dew.
Breakfast banter, jam on toast,
Our laughter rings; it's what we boast.

With mismatched chairs and silly hats,
We talk like cats, and dance like rats.
Imagined quirks in every meal,
Togetherness is how we feel.

The stereo plays our favorite song,
We carry on, we can't go wrong.
Tickled ribs, we guffaw out loud,
In these moments, we are proud.

So grab a joke, let's share a laugh,
In this chorus, there's no half.
With every heartbeat, with every cheer,
Love's melody is always near.

## **Giggles in the Breeze**

Whispers rustle through the grass,
Bouncing laughter, each moment flies past.
Chasing bubbles, we skip and twirl,
Nature's giggle makes our hearts whirl.

With every misstep, joy ignites,
Stumbling clumsy, but oh, what sights!
The sun winks down on our playful spree,
As we dance silly, just you and me.

Little bees buzz, join in the fun,
Life's a circus, and we're the run.
Juggling dreams and pie on our face,
In each giggle, we find our place.

So let us play in this cheerful haze,
Embrace the odd in all our ways.
In every chuckle, take a chance,
With giggles, love leads the dance.

## Serenade of Sweet Moments

Potato sack races, we fall with glee,
Chasing the sunset, just you and me.
With ice cream smiles and rainbow sprinkles,
Life is sweeter in silly wrinkles.

We share our dreams like secret tales,
Building castles with paper sails.
Under fairies, we throw confetti,
In a whirl of joy, we are unsteady.

The lanterns glow as we lift our feet,
In this serenade, our laughter's the beat.
With every chuckle, love blooms bright,
Together we chase the starlit night.

So here's to the moments sweet and spry,
Let's paint the skies, just you and I.
In every giggle, in every hug,
Our hearts dance together, forever snug.

## Chords of Blissful Connection

In a room filled with giggles, we play,
Every joke a note in our unique way.
Tickled by stories of silly old time,
We dance in the light, feeling oh so prime.

Crazy antics and laughter take flight,
In our little world, everything feels right.
With each shared smile, our hearts intertwine,
Creating a melody, simply divine.

## **Laughter's Gentle Caress**

A tickle, a punchline, a wink in the air,
Brighten the day with a light-hearted glare.
We clutch our sides, as those quips appear,
With friends all around, it's joy that we steer.

Silly faces and playful disputes,
Twinkling humor in our everyday routes.
In this sweet moment, we laugh just because,
Life feels like magic, we pause and we buzz.

## Tapestry of Tender Glee

In the cauldron of chuckles, we simmer and stew,
Mixing joy and shenanigans, just me and you.
With every high note, our spirits ascend,
We weave through the laughter, hand in hand, my friend.

Witty remarks and some slips on the floor,
Create a tableau we simply adore.
In the warmth of our banter, we find pure delight,
Knitting our hearts in the fabric of light.

## **Rhythms of Radiant Togetherness**

With a bounce in our step, we chase down the sun,
Sharing the joy, oh what fun can be done!
Each silly dance brings the laughter alive,
Like bees buzzing sweet, in our hive we thrive.

Through whimsical tales, we weave and we play,
In this garden of joy, we blossom each day.
We twirl through the moments, so carefree and bold,
A treasure of giggles, more precious than gold.

## The Brightness of Shared Moments

In a room where giggles dance,
Every glance a playful chance.
With silly faces in the air,
We find joy beyond compare.

Coffee spills and loud, loud snorts,
We laugh at all our funny thoughts.
With whispered jokes that keep us light,
Each moment sparkles, pure delight.

Bouncing back from silly falls,
Sharing secrets through the walls.
Silly hats and clumsy prance,
In every moment, we advance.

So let us cherish, hand in hand,
The bright moments, oh so grand.
With laughter echoing through space,
We find our home in each embrace.

## Uplifted by Laughter's Tune

Tickled toes and sunny smiles,
Laughter stretches endless miles.
With punchlines flying through the air,
We lose our worries without care.

A chuckle here, a giggle there,
In every joke, there's love to share.
Each quirky act, a joyful spark,
In the whispers of the park.

Nonsense turned to soaring flight,
Floating high on sheer delight.
With friends who lift us when we're down,
Our hearts expand; we wear a crown.

So here's to laughter, loud and bright,
That turns the mundane into light.
As harmony fills our happy crew,
We sing a tune both sweet and true.

## The Alchemy of Joyful Encounters

Through silly anecdotes we weave,
A tapestry we won't believe.
With laughter stitched in every seam,
We craft a world that feels like dream.

When friends arrive, the fun ignites,
With playful banter, pure delights.
Every moment, a jester's grace,
Finding humor in every space.

Whimsical stories come alive,
In funny twists, we all survive.
Through playful tricks and goofy pranks,
We fill our hearts and raise our ranks.

So gather 'round, let's share a jest,
For in our laughter, we are blessed.
Together, we create our art,
In this joyful dance, we never part.

## Musical Journey of Friendship

With laughter ringing like a bell,
In shared harmony, we dwell.
Silly songs and hearty roars,
Friendship opens countless doors.

As we trip through jokes like kids,
Every chat, a chance to bid.
We dance between the lines of glee,
With each note, we feel so free.

Odd impressions, playful strums,
In every heart, the laughter drums.
From funny tales of wacky days,
Our bond grows stronger in sonorous plays.

So let's embrace this joyous ride,
With laughter always by our side.
For in each moment that we seize,
Friendship hums with joyful ease.

## **Glistening Laughter in the Moonlight**

Under the silver beams, we play,
Giggling like kids at the end of the day.
With shadows dancing, spirits bright,
Our chuckles echo into the night.

Fireflies join our lively dance,
In this moment, we take a chance.
Whispers of joy cross the air,
In every giggle, love's found there.

The moon grins wide, a cheeky friend,
In this laughter, troubles bend.
Jokes spun like cotton candy sweet,
With each chuckle, our hearts skip a beat.

So let the nights be filled with mirth,
Rediscovering joy, oh what a worth.
As laughter twinkles in the skies,
Together, we find paradise.

## Vibrations of Lovingly Shared Laughter

Tickles and jests, the best of times,
Every pun wrapped in silly rhymes.
With your smirk brightening the gloom,
Our laughter fills every room.

Slapstick moments, tripping feet,
The way you fumble is quite the treat.
Snickers and snorts, we can't contain,
In silly antics, love's our gain.

Pranks that surprise, giggles galore,
Who knew we'd have so much in store?
Each laugh a bond that ties us tight,
A harmony of joy, pure delight.

So let the air ring with cheer,
In our laughter, there's nothing to fear.
A melody of joy we compose,
In each chuckle, our affection grows.

# The Joy Anthem

Bubbles and giggles fill the air,
With silly faces made without a care.
In the circus of life, we take our seat,
Juggling with joy, every heartbeat.

Chortles erupt like popcorn so bright,
As jokes bounce off the walls of the night.
Each snapshot captured like a gleeful show,
With laughter as the star, we let it flow.

Silly dances that make us grin,
With every twist, we pull each other in.
A chorus of glee in the evening breeze,
Our hearts sing louder than the tallest trees.

So let us strike up this joyful tune,
With every chuckle, we bounce like a balloon.
Together we'll write this song of delight,
With laughter, we shine, oh what a sight!

## The Wooing of Light and Laughter

In the glow of dawn, the fun begins,
With playful nudges and friendly spins.
Sunlight giggles as it breaks the morn,
In our hearts, happy smiles are born.

A dance of shadows, all in jest,
Where every snicker puts joy to the test.
Witty banter swings like a breeze,
In this get-together, we aim to please.

Puns and grins start painting the walls,
Laughter echoes in splendid halls.
A tickle here, a roguish glance,
In every moment, we find romance.

So let's woo the day with playful cheer,
Our laughter chimes, love draws near.
In this merry chase, we'll always find,
A treasure of joy that's intertwined.

## Chasing Joyful Echoes

In the garden of giggles, we dance,
Tickling the breeze in a playful trance.
Jesters in bloom, with hearts all aglow,
Chasing the echoes of laughter in tow.

With every shared glance, a joke takes flight,
Fireflies of humor, casting soft light.
Bubbles of joy bounce on hint of dawn,
Each chuckle we share, a new crown we don.

Through puddles of puddles, we leap and we slide,
Catching the sunshine, on this playful ride.
In a hat made of daisies, I fashion a crown,
And twirl like a fool, till I tumble down.

Chasing the twilight with smirks and with grins,
Our hearts filled with glee, as the music begins.
In the echoes of magic, together we soar,
With love that's contagious, who could ask for more?

## A Touch of Whimsical Love

In a land where the silliest dreams come true,
Where marshmallows giggle and umbrellas too.
A pickle in hand, we toast to the sky,
While the moon whispers secrets, oh my oh my!

With socks that don't match, we sashay on the street,
Two clowns on a mission with laughter so sweet.
Cupcakes on our heads, we're kings and queens,
In a court filled with jellybeans and jellybeans.

Each wink shared like candy, bright and absurd,
In this waltz of delights, we won't say a word.
With a twist of the wrist, and a spin of the heart,
We create a spectacle, a whimsical art.

So let's paint the world with our giggly glue,
Where love plays the lute and the jesters are true.
In this circus of joy, we frolic and roll,
Each laugh, a balloon, filling up our soul.

## Sweet Soundscapes of Joy

In the playground of whispers, our giggles collide,
With pancakes for hats, we take a wild ride.
A slide made of laughter, a swing of delight,
As we soar through the air, hearts light as a kite.

With slippery banana peels strewn on the ground,
We tumble with joy, collecting the sound.
In a symphony crafted from snickers and grins,
We dance with the quirks that light up our chins.

A tickle fight raging like thunder and rain,
With cupcakes that sprinkle sweet joy on our pain.
As the sun melts away, we will twirl and spin,
In a whirlwind of chuckles, let the fun begin!

So let's cherish the moments wrapped up in a hug,
As we skip through the gardens of moments that plug
Into hearts full of warmth and playful delight,
In sweet soundscapes of joy, we'll dance through the night.

## **Radiance in Every Smile**

In a world where chuckles bloom,
And giggles dance beneath the moon.
With every joke, we light the night,
In joy we find our pure delight.

Through silly faces, grins so wide,
Our laughter echoes, side by side.
With quirky tales and playful cheer,
We weave our joy, the world can hear.

A tickle here, a wink, a nudge,
In every smile, we're the fudge.
With love that sparkles, shines so bright,
In every laugh, we take our flight.

So let us cradle, every jest,
In playful hearts, we build our nest.
Together, hand in hand, we roam,
In laughter's glow, we find our home.

## The Sweet Laughter Tapestry

A tapestry of giggles spun,
With threads of joy, we have our fun.
In every knot, a tale unfolds,
A funny story, laughter holds.

With every pun, we twist and twine,
Share silly moments, hearts align.
Our laughter threads through day and night,
In giggly dreams, we take our flight.

From puns to quirks, our hearts ignite,
A purely joyous, playful sight.
Every chuckle we share sublime,
In harmony, we laugh through time.

So gather close, let laughter ring,
In silly tales, our spirits sing.
With each fond giggle, warmth we find,
As joy, like laughter, threads our mind.

## **Enchanting Lullabies of Us**

As twilight whispers, soft and sweet,
We share our giggles, hearts in beat.
In bedtime stories, joy takes flight,
With playful dreams, we greet the night.

Each chuckle woven, tender care,
A playful tale in moonlit air.
With every rhyme, our spirits soar,
In lullabies, we laugh for more.

Through funny sounds and soft embraces,
We find our peace in silly places.
Wrapped in warmth, with laughter's glow,
Together, through the world we flow.

So close your eyes, let joy unfold,
In dreams, our laughter will be told.
In every note, our love will shine,
As we create our sweet design.

## Whispers of Uplifting Love

In gentle whispers, laughter calls,
Like sunny rays that break the falls.
With teasing glances and playful winks,
In love's sweet dance, our heart syncs.

Beneath the stars, our jokes take flight,
In every punchline, pure delight.
From silly puns to playful schemes,
In laughter's warmth, we chase our dreams.

With mischievous grins, we talk and play,
In our own language, come what may.
Each giggle shared, a tender spark,
Together we write our joyful arc.

So lean in close, let laughter grow,
In every smile, we brightly glow.
With every jest, our hearts entwine,
In cozy moments, love's design.

## **Echoes of Delight**

In the garden, giggles bloom,
A butterfly slips in the room,
With tickles and whispers that chase,
Joy dances, paints every face.

Bubbles rise, wobbly and bold,
Chasing laughter, bright and cold,
With puppy eyes and silly prance,
Life turns into a joyful dance.

Every joke sung in the air,
Silly hats, a friend's great hair,
Funnier than a clown at play,
Moments that sweep our cares away.

## The Laughing Canvas

Colors splash with every laugh,
Silly art, a crazy craft,
Brushes twirl like dancers free,
Creating joy for all to see.

Paint drips down with giggles bright,
Funny faces, pure delight,
A canvas of our playful scene,
Where every hue makes us keen.

Splatters tell of stories bold,
In colors rich, our joy unfolds,
With every stroke, a chuckle rings,
In our hearts, the laughter springs.

## **Floating on Waves of Joy**

On the sea of smiles we sail,
With playful winds that tease and wail,
Every splash, a giggle's call,
In our boat, we're having a ball.

Seagulls cackle, riding high,
While we toss our worries shy,
Jumping waves with hearts so light,
Our laughter echoes, pure delight.

Drifting on this ocean spree,
Finding joy in silly glee,
With every wave, a jest unfolds,
In this tale, laughter beholds.

**The Sweet Symphony of Us**

In the kitchen, pots do sing,
As flour flies on joyful wing,
Mixing dreams in bowls so wide,
Together we bake with laughter's pride.

Cookies giggle on the sheet,
Silly shapes that can't be beat,
Frosting smiles, oh what a sight,
Every treat brings pure delight.

With stories wrapped in every bite,
We gather close, our hearts feel light,
In laughter's warmth, we find our home,
In the sweetness of us, we roam.

## Notes of Togetherness

In a room filled with giggles, we sway,
Hearts dance lightly, come what may.
Tickles and whispers, a playful tease,
Joyful laughter drifts on the breeze.

Mismatched socks and silly hats,
Frolicking cats where the fun is at.
Cupcakes with sprinkles, a frosting fight,
Each messy moment feels just right.

Counting clouds with ice cream cones,
Sharing stories in our yard of stones.
A chorus of chuckles, a delightful song,
In this melody, we all belong.

Together we stumble, we twirl, we fall,
With every bright smile, we conquer it all.
Life's silly moments, we'll cherish and note,
In the spell of our laughter, we float.

## The Crescendo of Warmth

Under the stars, our shadows blend,
Jokes and laughter, they never end.
The tickle fights erupt, oh dear!
Each chuckle shared warms like a cheer.

Mirthful moments, a game of chase,
With silly faces in our embrace.
A gentle shove, a playful shove,
In this joyful dance, we mold our love.

Beneath the moon, we find our beat,
With each laugh, our hearts compete.
Comedic tales from days long past,
These treasured memories forever last.

In this symphony of joy we find,
A tapestry woven, hearts entwined.
A heightening crescendo, the night ignites,
Together we sparkle, with love that delights.

## **Playful Rhythms**

Silly rhythms fill the air,
Jumping around without a care.
We groove and twist, with laughter free,
Chasing the moments, just you and me.

A waltz of mischief, a hop, a skip,
On this journey, let's take a trip.
With every giggle, the world's less bleak,
In our rhythm, the joy we seek.

Giggling echoes from kitchen delight,
Dancing with spoons, it feels so right.
Each outer space leap that we take,
In the universe of fun, we make.

With friends around, the music flows,
Magic in every step, it grows.
In our playful dance, we live unbound,
With laughter and love, our hearts are crowned.

## **Heartbeats in Unison**

As laughter rings, our hearts collide,
In the glow of joy, we take a ride.
Side by side in this merry race,
Each moment twinkling with a smiling face.

Bouncing ideas like balloons in flight,
Funny tales that sparkle so bright.
With every chuckle, we loosen the seams,
In the fabric of fun, we weave our dreams.

Unexpected slips on a banana peel,
Squeals of laughter, oh what a deal!
In these shenanigans, the bond we hold,
A story of warmth, together retold.

With heartbeats matching, we find our way,
In goofy dances, we laugh and sway.
With every shared grin, a promise anew,
In this journey of fun, it's me and you.

## **Notes of Playful Spirits**

In a garden of giggles, we play,
With shadows that dance in the sun's ray.
A tickle here, a jest there,
Each moment a treasure we share.

Mischief bounces like a ball,
We stumble and trip, yet never fall.
With silly hats and silly shoes,
The world is ours, we can't lose.

Laughter rolls like a sweet breeze,
Catching our breath, it's sure to please.
With every hiccup of delight,
We turn the mundane to pure light.

So come and join this wild spree,
Where jokes are as free as the sea.
In the melody of chuckles and cheer,
We find warmth in those we hold dear.

# The Warmth of Shared Laughter

Under the stars, our secrets flow,
With whispers and giggles, we steal the show.
A silly pop, a funny face,
In this little world, we find our place.

The sun peeks out with a playful grin,
We're off on a chase, let the fun begin.
With ice cream drips and silly games,
We humour the moments, we forget the names.

In every jest, there's a spark so bright,
Chasing shadows in the moonlit night.
Each roar of laughter, a sweet embrace,
In this joyful dance, we find our pace.

Friends around, the warmth is real,
In every chuckle, we heal and feel.
So let us toast with lemonade glee,
To laughter that binds you and me.

## Sweet Harmonies in the Air

A chorus of giggles fills the space,
As we intertwine in this playful chase.
With silly songs and whispers light,
We twirl in joy, our hearts take flight.

The wind joins in, a gentle tease,
As petals flutter down from the trees.
With each note sung, we craft our tune,
The moon winks at us, a merry boon.

Jokes hinted here, and laughter shared,
In the tapestry of moments prepared.
With every snort and playful shove,
We stitch together our tale of love.

So come let's dance till the stars fade away,
In the rhythm of joy, we choose to stay.
With laughter ringing through the night,
We celebrate this pure delight.

## Musical Echoes of Joy

With every giggle, a beat begins,
In a world where dance let's everyone win.
A sprinkle of fun, a dash of cheer,
Together we echo, the sound's so clear.

Through puddles we jump, with shoes full of mud,
Making memories, finding our flood.
In every chuckle, the magic remains,
Connecting our hearts like sweet refrains.

So grab a friend and spin around,
In the playground of life, joy is profound.
With each silly story and foolish glance,
We compose a tune in this wild dance.

With laughter as our guiding light,
We paint the world in colors so bright.
Echoes of joy fill the air we share,
In the symphony of life, we find our flair.

## **Hearts in Perfect Key**

In a room full of jest, we giggle away,
With mischief and giggles, we brighten the day.
Tickles and snickers make our spirits soar,
All worries forgotten, we laugh even more.

A pie in the face, a dance gone askew,
Each moment's a treasure, shared by the crew.
We tumble like clowns, in a world made of cheer,
With laughter our language, we have nothing to fear.

Sing out the jokes, let the punchlines be bright,
We're wrapped in a hug of wild sheer delight.
Faces aglow, like stars in the night,
In this merry affair, everything feels right.

So here we are, with spirit and zest,
Creating a magic that always feels best.
With laughter our glue, we'll never fall apart,
This joyful connection, the beat of our heart.

## **Harmony of Joyful Hearts**

Giggling together, we skip through the hours,
Like flowers in spring, bursting forth with powers.
A wink here, a smile, and the silliness flies,
Spreading the joy like confetti in skies.

Each quirk and odd joke, a cheerful embrace,
In the dance of our laughter, we find our own grace.
With antics aplenty, and silly charades,
We weave up our tales, like beautifully braids.

The tickle of laughter flows freely and fast,
Moments like these, we wish they would last.
From pratfalls to puns, we're a riotous crew,
In this joyful connection, love steadily grew.

So raise up your voice, let the chuckles entwine,
In the garden of humor, our hearts will align.
With beats that are golden and smiles that will shine,
We create our own melody, sweet and divine.

## The Melody of Smiles

Like notes from a tune, our laughter takes flight,
Sprinkling the air with joy, pure and bright.
A wink and a nod, we share in the fun,
With jokes tossed around like rays from the sun.

We prance through the chaos with rhythm and ease,
Giggling and grinning, we do as we please.
Swirls of delight in a whirlwind of cheer,
In this concert of joy, our hearts draw near.

With each hearty laugh, a new story ignites,
Transforming the mundane into pure delights.
Echoes of happiness bounce off the walls,
As we spin in this dance, where laughter enthralls.

So lift up your heart, let the music unfold,
In the orchestra of laughter, we all play bold.
Together we compose a tune ever sweet,
In this playful embrace, life feels complete.

## Dance of Delightful Whispers

In the corners we giggle, sharing our schemes,
Building up laughter from the silliest dreams.
With whispers of joy that tickle the air,
Every moment together, we savor and share.

With a hop and a skip, we leap into play,
Trading our secrets in the most goofy way.
A mischievous grin, and a wink, oh so sly,
In this dance of delight, we reach for the sky.

The world is our stage, make no mistake,
With cartoons and capers, we shake and we quake.
In the giggle-fueled moments, time swiftly flies,
Together we create our comedy prize.

So come join the revel, let silliness reign,
With laughter and love, we'll always regain.
In steps of humility, we spin and we twirl,
In this waltz of pure joy, we echo and whirl.

## Joyous Echoes

In the park, we chase the breeze,
Giggling under swaying trees.
With ice cream drips and playful fights,
Chasing dreams on sunny heights.

Tickles shared on a whimsical ride,
Laughter flows like a joyful tide.
As birds chirp notes of silly cheer,
We find delight in those we hold dear.

Frogs leap high, our shadows dance,
Every glance sparks a new chance.
With silly voices, we create a show,
Our hearts aglow, laughter in tow.

At sunset's glow, our tales unfold,
In moments rich, more precious than gold.
With each chuckle, the world stands still,
An echo of joy, a heart that will.

## The Dance of Merriment

In a room filled with jesters' flair,
Silly hats and antics to spare.
Dancing feet in mismatched shoes,
Twirling with giggles, our souls let loose.

Through twilight laughter, we sway and spin,
A charade of joy that draws us in.
With every stomp, the floor begins to creak,
Our hearts align, these moments we seek.

Balloons float high, caught in delight,
Whispers of fun echo through the night.
With playful claps and a cheery song,
We celebrate where we all belong.

The moonlight shines, our spirits soar,
In laughter's arms, we yearn for more.
With silly steps, we cherish the bliss,
The dance of merriment, a joyful kiss.

## **Whispers of Affection**

Amidst the giggles, secrets take flight,
Soft whispers shared beneath the starlight.
With a wink and a smile, we seal our pact,
In our little garden, joy is intact.

Silly stories spun with delight,
We laugh till it hurts, hearts feeling light.
With every quip and playful tease,
We find warmth in moments that please.

Under the blanket of a midnight sky,
We paint the stars and let our dreams fly.
With hearts wide open, love's gentle glow,
In this silly dance, our spirits flow.

As laughter lingers, evening drifts near,
In the cradle of mirth, all feels clear.
Whispers of affection fill the spaces,
In every smile, the joy embraces.

## **Melodies in the Heart**

A tickle here, a poke right there,
Life's little tunes, we're free as air.
With playful jests that hum through the day,
We find our rhythm, come what may.

In a whirlwind of joy, our spirits align,
Silly serenades, each moment a sign.
With laughter's verse, we craft our song,
In this lighthearted world, we all belong.

Every chuckle ignites the night,
Melodies soar, everything feels right.
With eyes that twinkle and hearts that gleam,
Together we laugh, together we dream.

As dawn breaks forth, our stories combine,
A ballad of friendships that brightly shine.
In the echo of joy, love finds its way,
In melodies sung, come what may.

## Laughter's Gentle Reverie

In a world where chuckles reign,
Giggles sprinkle like soft rain,
Mirth dances in the sunny breeze,
Where worries fade and hearts feel free.

Bubbling over like soda pop,
Each joke's a cherry, never stop,
Smiles exchanged like currency,
A treasure trove of memory.

Ticklish moments shared with friends,
Laughter's echo never ends,
Whimsical tales weave through the air,
With every grin, we shed our care.

Joyful whispers, secrets spun,
In this realm, we are all one,
With skirts of bliss and shoes of fun,
We waltz beneath the glowing sun.

## The Bright Chime of Love

A gentle tease, a playful jest,
In hearts that twirl, we feel our best,
Each giggle a note in our song,
Together we dance, where we belong.

Witty banter, a lively game,
With every laugh, it's never the same,
Like coffee sipped on a lazy morn,
In our laughter, new joys are born.

Whispers of joy in every look,
Entwined like pages in a book,
A punchline here, a wink right there,
In this rhythm of love, we share.

Moments of bliss, like stardust glow,
With every quip, our spirits flow,
In this melody of hearts unfurled,
We craft our own bright, loving world.

## **Whirlwind of Joyful Spirits**

In a whirl of giggles, we take flight,
Spirits soaring, hearts so light,
Tickles and laughter in every turn,
Through joy and jest, we brightly burn.

Crazy dances in silly shoes,
We twirl and tumble, casting blues,
With every fall, a hearty laugh,
In this joyous chaos, we find our path.

Jokes like confetti, brightly strewn,
Under the glow of a laughing moon,
Where fun and frolics never cease,
In this flutter, we find our peace.

Side by side, through thick and thin,
With every chuckle, we always win,
A whirlwind of joy, with smiles we paint,
In this canvas of life, we place our claim.

## The Hug of Happiness

Wrapped in warmth like a cozy quilt,
A squeeze so tight, no space is built,
With laughter bubbling like a stream,
In each embrace, we live the dream.

Beneath the stars, we spin and sway,
In joy's embrace, we play all day,
With whispered jokes and silly quips,
In every hug, our happiness grips.

With open hearts, we share the glee,
Each hug's an invitation to be free,
Like sunshine spilling through the trees,
We bask in love, with playful ease.

In this circle of laughter, we belong,
Together we sing our playful song,
So take my hand, and let's not part,
For every hug is a work of art.

## **Celebrating the Art of Joy**

In a world of chuckles bright,
We dance with joy, hearts in flight.
With every giggle, smiles abound,
In this merry land, we're joyfully crowned.

Tickles twist in playful glee,
As laughter flows, wild and free.
We wear our jokes like hats of cheer,
Bringing warmth to all that's near.

With silly songs, we sway and spin,
In this game of joy, we all win.
Each playful moment, a treasure to keep,
Where hearty laughs run deep and steep.

So join the dance, let your spirit soar,
In the art of joy, we find even more.
With hugs and smiles, we'll play our part,
In this joyful canvas, we paint our heart.

## Notes from the Heart's Orchestra

With a playful quirk and a wink so sly,
We strum the chords of laughter high.
The flutes of mirth sound light and clear,
In the concert of hearts, we draw near.

Bouncing beats from jovial drums,
Bring forth the joy, the giggles, the hums.
With every note, a grin we share,
Creating magic, beyond compare.

The banter flows like a gentle stream,
In this playful space, we find our dream.
With each chord struck, the mood takes flight,
We're crafting symphonies through the night.

So raise your voice, let laughter play,
In this heart's orchestra, come what may.
Together we stand, in joyful embrace,
Crafting memories we'll never erase.

## The Lullaby of Shared Dreams

When stars twinkle in the night,
We share our dreams, pure delight.
With giggles soft as the moon's light,
Our hopes take wing, in joyous flight.

In the realm where giggles bloom,
We chase away any hint of gloom.
With whispered tales beneath the sky,
We crack up dragons that fly too high.

Each lullaby wrapped in delight,
Makes every moment feel just right.
We dream in colors, bright and loud,
Together we shine, forever proud.

With snickers sweet like candy canes,
We'll tickle the moon with our joyous refrains.
In this lullaby, our hearts will weave,
A tapestry of dreams that we believe.

## Cadence of Carefree Hearts

In fields of daisies, we frolic and play,
Embracing laughter, come what may.
With carefree hearts and playful strides,
In the dance of joy, love abides.

We skip through puddles, splash and cheer,
Every droplet brings us near.
With jokes and jests, we laugh with glee,
In this carefree world, we're truly free.

Around the fire, stories we tell,
With laughter echoing a joyful bell.
We toss our worries to the breeze,
Finding peace with playful ease.

As stars peek down and smile on us,
We're wrapped in warmth, in laughter's trust.
In this rhythm where hearts entwine,
The cadence of joy, forever divine.

## Serenading Sunlit Moments

In the park where shadows play,
Children's giggles float away.
A dog in socks, he prances neat,
Chasing tails with dancing feet.

Ice cream drips on sun-kissed skin,
A clown slips down, the laughter's win.
Balloons are flying, colors swirl,
A day like this, it makes us twirl.

Ticklish grass beneath our toes,
As silly faces bloom like prose.
A silly hat atop my head,
In these moments, joy is spread.

Rainbows drawn with chalk and cheer,
Our laughter echoes, bright and clear.
The sun winks down, it knows the score,
In sunny places, who wants more?

## The Lightness of Laughter

With every joke that brings a smile,
We float above the worries, awhile.
A parrot talks, a puppet sings,
Life's laughter, oh, the joy it brings!

Bananas in pajamas dance in line,
Silly slips—what a grand design!
A tickle monster roams about,
With gleeful shrieks and merry shout.

As goofy faces paint the air,
The world seems light, without a care.
When friends all gather, jesters too,
The lighter hearts, we'll see it through.

With every pun and gleeful rhyme,
We laugh together, lost in time.
A tumble here, a slip, a slide,
In humor's warmth, we all abide.

## **Delight in Every Beat**

A dance of joy, we shimmy close,
With every beat, a lively dose.
The silly hat atop my brow,
Who knew fun wore a grin like now?

Laughter leaps from every side,
In this playground, we take our ride.
Sing like frogs in a pond, oh dear,
Our silly antics draw us near.

Tap dancing feet on dandelions,
Comedic sparks, our hearts' refiners.
With wobbly steps yet joyous glee,
Our laughter echoes, wild and free.

In blissful rhythms, our souls unite,
The sound of smiles, pure and bright.
With every chuckle, life's a game,
In the dance of joy, we're all the same.

## Whispers of Joyful Connection

A secret shared beneath the stars,
With laughter twinkling like guitars.
In every glance, a spark ignites,
In playful moments, love takes flight.

We giggle soft, a whispered jest,
In cozy nooks, we feel the best.
A tickle fight, some friendly tease,
In these sweet times, our hearts find ease.

The warmth of friends, an airy tune,
Under the glow of a bright full moon.
Silly stories that make us cry,
In bonds of laughter, we fly high.

With whispered secrets, soft and light,
In every joke, our worlds feel bright.
A dance of joy, under skies so wide,
In playful whispers, love's our guide.

## The Jubilant Waltz

In the dance of our silly strides,
Joy twirls where giggles abide.
Each step a chuckle, a wink, a tease,
The world feels lighter with such ease.

With two left feet, we spin and fall,
But in your eyes, I find it all.
A misstep here, a shuffle there,
Together clumsy, nothing to spare.

We leap like frogs, we glide like air,
In this rhythm, there's hardly a care.
Two hearts beat wild, a carefree plume,
In laughter's embrace, we find our room.

So let's waltz on through life's bright maze,
Each giggle turning to playful praise.
Amidst our stumbles, the joy remains,
In every laugh, our love sustains.

## Blossoms of Playful Affection

Petals fall from our silly grins,
As laughter bursts like winter's winds.
Tickles and teasing, a playful race,
Our hearts blossom in this space.

In puddles, we splash like carefree kids,
Finding joy in each little bid.
With every tumble, our spirits rise,
Our playful banter, a sweet surprise.

Each wink we share, a secret bloom,
In this garden where we consume.
A fragrance of fun fills the air,
Together in mischief, love we declare.

Through silly jokes and bright bouquet,
Our playful affection finds its way.
In laughter's arms, we surely thrive,
In this dance of joy, we come alive.

## **Notes of Togetherness**

In a world filled with jests and glee,
Your laughter sings a melody.
Each chuckle shared, a perfect note,
In the chorus of love, we happily float.

Like playful birds, we chirp and cheer,
Creating symphonies, crystal clear.
With every snort and silly sound,
In this sweet music, joy is found.

A tickle here, a giggle there,
In our duet, we have no care.
Together we hum, our hearts in tune,
Under the watchful gaze of the moon.

In this cacophony, our love aligns,
With laughter ringing through the pines.
Our song's a dance of pure delight,
In the notes of us, the world feels right.

## The Rhythm of Shared Journeys

With each adventure, we take a leap,
In laughter's embrace, the memories we keep.
Through winding roads and silly trails,
Together we soar like joyful gales.

In funny hats and playful masks,
We find the fun in every task.
Side by side with hearts so bold,
In your laughter, I find my gold.

Through ups and downs, we hold on tight,
With each shared grin, we ignite the night.
In the rhythm of our joyful chase,
Life's a ballet, a wondrous space.

So let's roam free with giggling glee,
In this dance of love, just you and me.
Together we'll write our whimsical song,
In the rhythm of laughter, we belong.

## Heartstrings of Shared Laughter

In the park where giggles grow,
Tickling winds put on a show.
Silly hats on wobbly heads,
Frogs sing songs from leafy beds.

Joyful dances, clumsy and bright,
Chasing shadows into the night.
Laughs like bubbles float in the sky,
Moments together just zipped by.

Whispers of puns shared with glee,
Ticklish secrets, just you and me.
Clowns with shoes way too big,
Making us laugh, oh what a jig!

Under stars, our giggles twine,
Crafting joy like sweet red wine.
In this tale where laughter rings,
Love blooms loud, and laughter sings.

## Exultation in Every Smile

The sun peeks through silly faces,
Radiates joy in warm embraces.
Puppies prance in joyful leaps,
Finding the laughter that never sleeps.

Each wink a secret, each grin a clue,
Silly dances, me and you.
Slips and trips, oh what a show,
With every tumble, more joy flows.

Chasing each other round and round,
Giggling echoes abound, abound.
A tea party with frogs in hats,
Nonsense piled high, where fun's at!

Count the chuckles, count the cheers,
Filling our hearts with happy years.
In our fortress of pure delight,
Love sparkles in the starry night.

## The Canvas of Shared Happiness

Splashing colors on a bright day,
Dancing crayons, in a playful way.
Funny monsters with silly grins,
Paint the world where laughter spins.

Bubblegum skies and jellybean trees,
Giggles float on the gentle breeze.
Twirling joy through happy streets,
Every step, the rhythm beats.

Tickled pink, we break the mold,
Funny stories just waiting to unfold.
Paint the canvas, laughter flows,
In our hearts, where magic grows.

Mirthful moments brush the air,
Creating joy, beyond compare.
On this art of laughter drawn,
Love forever humming on.

## Love's Silken Soundtrack

On a stage of jester's play,
Ticklish tunes lead the way.
Every note a giggle bright,
Moments wrapped in pure delight.

Dancing shadows, whispers shared,
Love's music plays, unprepared.
Silly hats and mismatched shoes,
Every step, we choose to muse.

A heart that sings, a smile that glows,
Together through life, the laughter flows.
With every harmony, joy we weave,
In this song, we believe.

A playful rhythm, a joyful sigh,
Under the sun, we soar and fly.
In this melody where we belong,
Love's friendly tune plays strong and long.

## Echoes of Affection

Tickles and giggles fill the air,
Playful whispers without a care.
A joke shared under a starlit sky,
Laughter dances, oh my, oh my!

Silly faces and playful pouts,
In this game, there are no doubts.
Catch a smirk, then run away,
Who knew love could be this silly today?

Chaos reigns in our tiny nook,
Spilled popcorn and a shared book.
With each chuckle, our hearts collide,
Together forever, side by side.

In the echoes of affection, we play,
Turning mundane into a holiday.
With each shared glance and all the fun,
Our bond blossoms, two becoming one.

## Serenade of Shared Secrets

Under blankets, we whisper and tease,
Inside jokes that bring us to our knees.
You snort when I laugh, oh such a sight,
The world seems dimmer without our light.

Bubblegum pop and silly songs,
In this duet, nothing feels wrong.
Tickle fights turn to gentle sighs,
Laughter echoes, a joyful surprise.

Balcony chats with stars in our eyes,
Stumbling over our twisted lies.
With our secrets, we paint the night,
Together, always, you feel so right.

The serenade of hearts intertwined,
In laughter and whispers, love we find.
Hold my hand, let's dance the night through,
In this symphony, it's just me and you.

## Crescendo of Cheerful Moments

From pancakes flipped to cats that prance,
Every misstep turns into a dance.
With sticky fingers and cream on our face,
Life's little blunders become our embrace.

Running in circles, we chase the sun,
Each moment cherished, oh so fun!
Funny faces at the mirror's glance,
In this wacky world, we take a chance.

Unexpected twists in our joyful ride,
With hearts wide open, let's just abide.
A slip, a laugh, a spark of delight,
In this crescendo, everything feels right.

So let's collect these moments dear,
In fits of giggles, we hold each other near.
With every laugh, our love does bloom,
In this silly dance, there's always room.

## **The Song of Embraced Souls**

In a world of chaos, we find our tune,
With ticklish whispers beneath the moon.
A bubble of joy wraps us tight,
In your laughter, the stars lie bright.

Quirky antics and inside jokes,
Finding humor in the oddest strokes.
With you, even silence has a beat,
In this symphony, life feels sweet.

Running late, but we laugh it off,
In this dance, we often scoff.
With mischief wrapped in loving flair,
We flip the mundane into the rare.

As embraced souls, our love takes flight,
Finding joy in the smallest delight.
With giggles and grins, we pave our way,
Hand in hand, come what may.

## The Lightness of Being

In a world of giggles and grins,
Floating like balloons in the winds,
Tickled by whispers, soft and sweet,
Dancing on laughter, life is a treat.

Silly antics under the sun,
Chasing shadows, oh what fun!
With each chuckle, hearts take flight,
Joy is found in the silliest sight.

Jokes tailing tails, the punchlines fly,
Twinkling eyes like stars in the sky,
Mirthful melodies fill the air,
Love entwined in each playful dare.

So let's twirl in this playful spree,
Where smiles ring out like a symphony,
In the lightness of being, we find our way,
Through laughter's embrace, come join the play!

## Chimes of Cherished Times

Bells of laughter ringing clear,
Tickling thoughts we hold so dear,
Each moment shared, a spark ignites,
Joy's sweet echo through starry nights.

Chasing after the playful breeze,
Giggling under the swaying trees,
Every glance a teasing game,
With love's soft touch, nothing's the same.

Silly stories, oh how they flow,
Like bubbles rising, sweet and slow,
In these chimes, our hearts align,
Crafting memories divine and fine.

So lift your voice, let laughter soar,
In cherished times, we long for more,
With every chuckle, let's toast tonight,
To the moments that make our souls feel bright!

**Blissful Resonance**

A quirky dance in the morning light,
Spreading cheer, oh what a sight,
With each burst of mirth, we play,
In blissful resonance, we seize the day.

Snorts and snickers fuel our cheer,
The world feels right when friends are near,
Laughter spills like a bubbling stream,
Together we craft the silliest dream.

Witty banter fills the air,
Joyful jests everywhere we share,
With every punchline, hearts entwine,
In this bliss, what joy we find!

So raise a glass filled with delight,
In laughter's glow, our spirits take flight,
Together we sing, let the good times flow,
In the echo of giggles, love's seeds will grow!

# Love Notes in the Air

Sweet whispers flutter like butterflies,
Joyful secrets shared, often surprise,
Every glance a note, soft and light,
In love's sweet dance, hearts take flight.

Jokes kissed by the playful breeze,
Ticklish moments that aim to please,
In the warmth of smiles, we find our way,
Crafting laughter to brighten the day.

With each chuckle, the world feels bright,
Painting our lives with pure delight,
Nonsense wrapped in affection's thread,
Creating melodies as words are said.

So let's serenade with hearts so true,
In this joyful song, it's me and you,
With love notes carried in laughter's sway,
Together we dance, come what may!

## The Dance of Lighthearted Love

In a garden where joy takes flight,
Hearts twirl beneath the moon's soft light,
Laughter bubbles like a sweet, fizzy drink,
Love pirouettes, making us think.

Silly faces and playful spins,
Each glance a game, where fun begins,
A leap, a hop, in a jovial race,
With giggles that paint smiles on each face.

Tickling fancies, a jester's call,
Together we rise, together we fall,
A silly dance, where we lose our way,
In this charmed night, forever we stay.

So let the music play oh-so-bright,
As we waltz through dream until morning light,
With every step, let the laughter ignite,
As love and mirth become our delight.

## Whimsical Waves of Happiness

On the beach where the giggles soar,
Waves of joy crash upon the shore,
A dance of sand, a splash of cheer,
In a sea of smiles, we have nothing to fear.

Kites in the sky, swirling around,
Each colorful flight a promise profound,
Caught in the breeze, like our laughs that fly,
With every whistle, the seagulls cry.

Jumping in puddles, splashing away,
As the sun sets low, brightening our play,
Whirls of whimsy in each twinkling eye,
A tide of joy, forever nearby.

In this playful space, let's sing and sway,
With every heartbeat, we float and play,
The waves of happiness, forever they stay,
Carrying love's whispers, day after day.

## Ensemble of Heartfelt Giggles

In the theater of hearts, the curtains rise,
A cast of characters with twinkling eyes,
We skip through acts with mischief and glee,
An ensemble of chuckles, as light as can be.

With feathers and wigs, we play our roles,
Silly antics and comedic goals,
Each line a punch, every scene a delight,
In this play of life, we shine ever bright.

A tickle here, an unexpected fall,
As laughter erupts, we savor it all,
With hearts conjoined, we sweep through the stage,
In this boundless tale, we unveil every page.

United in joy, we bow in response,
With cheers and applause in an endless dance,
Oh, what a show, how delightful the scene,
In this playful world, we reign as the queen.

## The Chorus of Kindred Spirits

In a circle of friends, we gather 'round,
The music of laughter is a joyous sound,
Voices harmonize in the warm summer air,
Kindred spirits, with stories to share.

From silly tales of mishaps and woe,
To wild adventures that only we know,
Each note a whisper, a memory bright,
Together we weave through day into night.

Tickling hearts with the lightest of glee,
Singing our praises to love, you and me,
With every chuckle, we dance through the day,
A chorus of joy that never will sway.

In this melody of friendship and cheer,
Each laugh a reminder that love is near,
With every refrain, may the laughter ring true,
In the song of our lives, it's me and it's you.

## Embrace of Laughter

Tickles and giggles fill the air,
Bumbling dances without a care.
Jokes inside jokes, oh what a sight,
Laughter erupts till the morning light.

Mismatched socks with a bright blue tie,
Funny faces that make you sigh.
Silly stories exchanged with glee,
Together we craft this wacky spree.

Bouncing around like a rubber ball,
A pie in the face, we embrace it all.
Time slips away on this merry ride,
In this joyful moment, we take pride.

From jokes to pranks, our hearts entwined,
With every laugh, a love defined.
This crazy world spins on its own,
In the warmth of humor, we've truly grown.

# **Tapestry of Joyful Hearts**

Weaving tales with threads of cheer,
Every chuckle draws us near.
With vibrant colors, we paint the day,
In laughter's light, we lose our way.

Cups of joy filled to the brim,
Giggling softly, the lights grow dim.
A slip on the floor, oh what a mess,
Yet in this chaos, we find our blessed.

In the kitchen, pots are stacked high,
A chef who can't cook yet aims for the sky.
From belly laughs to snorts of mirth,
In our joyful hearts, we find our worth.

One little poke, and off we fly,
Floating together, like clouds in the sky.
With each funny moment, we draw closer,
In this tapestry, love's our composer.

## The Rhythm of Connection

Dancing to beats made of snorts,
Twists and turns in our funny shorts.
A hop, skip, and a jump so wild,
In this quirky beat, we're like a child.

Mismatched rhythms make us grin,
As we twirl around, love's melody begins.
With every bump and stumble, we play,
In the joyful chaos, we find our way.

A wink shared across the room,
Like a flower in full bloom.
In our laughter, we find connection,
An endless dance in this affection.

Through tickling tunes and happy beats,
We march together, no retreat.
In this rhythm, hearts beat as one,
Laughter connects us—oh what fun!

## **Laughter's Gentle Song**

Whispers of joy rise like a breeze,
Jokes about ants and mischievous bees.
In a game of charades, we all can't mime,
Yet in our stumbles, we find the rhyme.

Bouncing notes of hearty cheer,
Echoing limits of what we hold dear.
A gentle poke brings out a shrill,
In this dance of giggles, we find the thrill.

Silly faces like rubber masks,
Unruly laughter—oh, what a task!
With every chuckle, love takes flight,
In laughter's melody, we feel just right.

As the stars twinkle, our hearts align,
In the symphony of the punchline.
Each note, a spark in the night,
In laughter's song, our spirits ignite.

## A Playful Interlude

In the garden of giggles, we play,
Chasing shadows, we dance all day.
With silly hats and twinkling eyes,
We sparkled like stars in the bright blue skies.

Lemonade spills, and laughter flows,
Tickling toes where the dandelion grows.
Each hiccup of joy, a note to sing,
In this sweet madness, we find our spring.

Whispers of mischief in every breeze,
We juggle our dreams with the greatest ease.
Banana peels slip, and the world spins round,
In this playful interlude, joy knows no bound.

With every chuckle and playful tease,
Life's a circus; we do as we please.
In the funhouse mirror of our delight,
We dance through the night, hearts shining bright.

# The Joyful Rhapsody

Two clowns in a tub, splashes abound,
Tickled pink laughter is all around.
With pies in our faces and joy in our hearts,
The music of chuckles, our life's sweetest arts.

Hearts leap like kangaroos in the sun,
Making silly faces just for fun.
A hop, a skip, through the daisies we run,
In the world of delight, we've already won.

Each tickle and tease a note in the air,
Harmonies rise with the laughter we share.
Skits of our lives dance in endless replay,
Creating a rhapsody brightening our day.

With every misstep, we burst into cheer,
In this vibrant melody, there's nothing to fear.
Just a rhythm of giggles echoing true,
In our joyful rhapsody, I find joy in you.

## The Radiant Song of Us

Underneath the moon, we skip and sway,
Our jests are the stars that light up the way.
With heart-shaped balloons and a wink of the eye,
We conquer the night, just you and I.

Each chuckle a note, each smile a rhyme,
We dance in the sparkles, defying all time.
The world is our stage, with no need for scripts,
Just laughter and love in whimsical flips.

Like pop songs we hum, with a twist and a twirl,
In this dance of delight, our hearts do unfurl.
Together we bloom like flowers in spring,
In the radiant song, our joy is the king.

With every embrace, the music grows strong,
In this melody sweet, we've finally found where we belong.
With love as our chorus, together we sing,
In the vibrant embrace of everything.

# The Harmonious Journey

On bicycles built for two we roam,
Through puddles of laughter, we find our home.
With each wobble and giggle, we sail through the day,
In the map of our joy, we'll find our way.

Riding clouds made of marshmallows and dreams,
Where everything's brighter than it truly seems.
With socks that don't match and ice cream galore,
Each moment a treasure, let's gather some more.

We leap through the puddles, our laughter a song,
In this quirky adventure, where we both belong.
With each twist and turn, we create our own tune,
In the harmonious journey, we'll dance with the moon.

Through sunny skies and rain, side by side,
With laughter so pure, there's nothing to hide.
In the joy of the journey, we find our delight,
Together forever, our hearts take flight.

## The Playful Waltz

In twirls of joy, we skip and sway,
With giggles bright, we dance away.
A poke, a tease, around we spin,
In laughter's grip, the fun begins.

With cheeky grins and silly hats,
We prance like clowns, and pounce like cats.
A twirling skirt, a laughing shout,
In every step, we twist about.

From kitchen floors to garden greens,
We leap with joy, like playful beans.
With friendly jabs and playful roles,
Our laughter's tune fondly rolls.

So let the world hear our delight,
As we dance through both day and night.
In every smile, a spark ignites,
In this sweet waltz, our hearts take flight.

## Revelry in the Moonlight

Beneath the stars, we dance and shout,
With moonlit beams that twist about.
The fireflies join, in sparkling cheer,
As whispers turn to raucous jeer.

With goofy grins and mischief's spark,
We play till dawn, from light to dark.
The night is young, let's make a mess,
In this sweet chaos, we find our bliss.

A limbo line, we bend and sway,
With every laugh, we drift away.
From clumsy moves to giant leaps,
Our joy, like night, forever keeps.

So toss your cares and join the fun,
In moonlit magic, we are one.
With hearts so light, let's sing it loud,
In revelry, we're truly proud.

## Joyful Cadences

With bouncy steps, we groove to cheer,
Each note a laugh that fills the air.
A rhythm built on silly sounds,
In happy beats, our joy abounds.

From silly songs to whacky rhymes,
We dance away the clunky times.
A step, a hop, a twirl so grand,
Side by side, we take our stand.

With giggles sweet like candy's bite,
Our jolly hearts ignite the night.
A playful jig, we leap and glide,
With laughter's warmth, we'll never hide.

So join the chorus, sing along,
In this wild tune, we all belong.
With joyful cadences, hand in hand,
In every beat, our hearts expand.

## Heartstrings in Harmony

With playful notes, we pluck and strum,
A melody that makes us hum.
With hearts entwined, we laugh and sing,
In sweet harmony, joy takes wing.

A tangle here, a mix-up there,
With music bright filling the air.
In every chord, a grin appears,
Our laughter rings through all the years.

With silly faces and joyful tones,
We float together, not alone.
With every laugh, we swell with pride,
In this warm bond, love won't hide.

So let's create this jubilant song,
In harmony, we all belong.
With heartstrings pulled and laughter high,
Together we reach for the sky.

## Playful Serenade of Us

In the garden of giggles, we twirl,
A whirlwind of joy, our hearts all a-whirl.
Each chuckle blooms like flowers of cheer,
Your smile, my sunshine, always so near.

With silly hats and shoes of great size,
We waddle and wobble beneath the blue skies.
Our secrets shared in whispers and quirks,
Creating a world where humor just works.

On swings we swing, with laughter so bright,
As gravity giggles, and takes our delight.
We race to the ice cream, a sticky delight,
Three scoops of joy, what a silly sight!

Together we dance, through puddles and rain,
Each splash is a note in our playful refrain.
Hand in hand, through this merry charade,
In our playful serenade, we serenely parade.

## The Blissful Connections

Balloons fly high, with giggles attached,
Each burst sparkles, like stars that we matched.
You tickle my thoughts, a joyous embrace,
In the maze of our laughter, we find our place.

Cups filled with cocoa, marshmallows afloat,
As we dream silly dreams, on this lighthearted boat.
Each sip comes with snorts, a brew of delight,
In this whimsical potion, all worries take flight.

We juggle our hopes, with a dash of the bold,
Turning mishaps to stories, forever retold.
With every slip and fall, we just break into cheer,
Finding bliss in connections that dry every tear.

In this dance of the quirky, our spirits unite,
As laughter, our soundtrack, banishes fright.
Through the bonds that we've woven, so carefree and pure,
In the blissful connections, our hearts feel secure.

## **Dances Under Moonlit Laughter**

Underneath the stars, we leap and we bound,
With giggles that echo, a magical sound.
The moon winks at us, in a playful tease,
As we shuffle about, and do as we please.

Crickets sing backup to our silly tunes,
While fireflies dance, under whimsical moons.
With every twirl, the night sky takes part,
In our silly dance, where we laugh from the heart.

We tiptoe around, on this soft grassy floor,
Wearing socks on our hands, who could ask for more?
Each step a delight, in this moonbeam affair,
Our laughter echoes, carried through the air.

The world fades away, in this joyful spree,
With laughter and love, just you, and just me.
In our moonlit escapade, we find endless cheer,
In a dance of pure joy, our hearts hold so dear.

## The Laughter Tapestry

Threads of our giggles, they weave and entwine,
A tapestry bright, with colors so fine.
Each knot full of stories, precious and rare,
In this fabric of fun, we find joy to share.

With pranks in our pockets, and wit in our sleeves,
We craft happy moments, as each one believes.
The world is our canvas, we splash it with glee,
In every mishap, there's magic, you see.

Through tickle fights and whispers, we stitch with delight,

Every hug a reminder, we're wrapped up so tight.
With laughter as glue, we hold this all fast,
Creating a tapestry, meant forever to last.

So here's to the joy, in the fun that we sow,
In the laughter mosaic, we endlessly grow.
Together we flourish, our stories combine,
In the lively creation, our hearts do align.

Milton Keynes UK
Ingram Content Group UK Ltd.
UKHW030751121124
451094UK00013B/791